Coconut and Licorice are such good friends.
They spend as much time together as they
possibly can. They love to play, but they also
like to learn more about each other.

This book is full of quizzes to help you learn
more about yourself and a special friend.
For every quiz, you'll find a pair—tear out
one for you and one to share!

Published by Pleasant Company Publications
Copyright © 2004 by American Girl, LLC

Questions or comments? Call 1-800-845-0005,
visit our Web site at **americangirl.com**,
or write American Girl, P.O. Box 620497, Middleton, WI 53562-0497.

Printed in China.
04 05 06 07 08 09 10 LEO 10 9 8 7 6 5 4 3 2 1

American Girl®, Coconut™, Licorice™, and the Coconut and Licorice designs and
logos are trademarks of American Girl, LLC.

Editorial Development: Elizabeth Chobanian, Sara Hunt, Michelle Watkins
Art Direction: Camela Decaire, Chris Lorette David
Design: Camela Decaire
Production: Kendra Pulvermacher, Mindy Rappe, Jeannette Bailey, Judith Lary
Illustrations: Casey Lukatz

Contents

Tear out both matching quizzes. Work on them at the same time with a friend.

Coconut™

Quizzes

for You

The sweetest treat is the smile of a friend.

Favorite Flavors

Coconut's favorite flavor of ice cream is Coconut Cream. Do you know what flavor is your friend's top pick? What about her least-likely-to-lick? Rank each flavor below for your friend, from first (#1) to worst (#6).

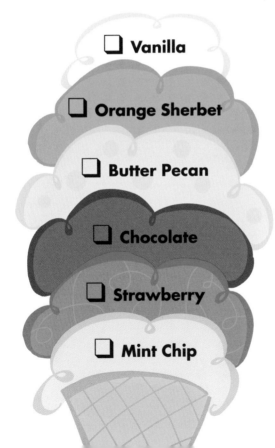

☐ **Vanilla**

☐ **Orange Sherbet**

☐ **Butter Pecan**

☐ **Chocolate**

☐ **Strawberry**

☐ **Mint Chip**

Answers

Ask your friend to check your answers to see how you did.
How many did you guess right?

One or two
Double Scoop Troop

There's plenty of time to learn more about each other. Why not spend an afternoon sharing stories about yourselves—while you share an ice cream sundae!

Three or four
Banana Split Sisters

You know a lot about your friend. But she still likes to surprise you sometimes. So many flavors, so little time!

Five or six
Whipped Cream Team

Your friend has no secrets from you—or have you two been to the ice cream shoppe together lately?

Dream On!

Sweet dreams? Not always. Dreams can also be silly, strange, or scary. Sometimes they represent what you're thinking or feeling. Check off any dreams below that you've had. Then read on to find out what your dreams might mean.

☐ **1. You're falling.**

☐ **2. You lost something.**

☐ **3. You're being chased.**

 4. You're flying.

5. A house

6. You're not wearing any clothes.

7. All your teeth fall out.

8. A storm

 BooM

10

Answers

1. You're falling.
Dreams of falling often mean that you're feeling uneasy or that someone has let you down. But did you know that people usually wake up before they hit bottom in their dreams?

2. You lost something.
If you dreamed about losing something, or if you were lost, you might be feeling like something is missing in your life. What do you think the lost item stands for?

3. You're being chased.
If you were running from something in a dream, chances are, you're trying to get away from something in your life. Have you been putting off some chores, or did you forget to do your homework?

4. You're flying.
How did you feel in your dream? If you felt happy, you're probably feeling on top of the world in real life. But if you were frightened in your dream, there might be something scary you wish you could get away from—like that upcoming piano recital!

11

5. A house

The house represents you. Was there a hidden room? Maybe you're keeping a secret in real life. Were the rooms all different colors? Maybe you have a flair for art or fashion.

6. You're not wearing any clothes.

Dreams about being naked have to do with your feelings—*not* your body. Perhaps in real life there's a thought or feeling that you'd like to keep under wraps?

7. All your teeth fall out.

This dream may seem weird, but lots of people have it. Usually it means there's something in your life that feels out of your control. Maybe your room is super messy, or your little brother has been bugging you.

8. A storm

Dreams about natural disasters are scary. They usually represent something in your life that is frightening you, too. A tornado, for example, may mean you're feeling out of control.

Here's to sweet dreams and starry skies!

Pal Poll

Coconut knows a lot about her friend Licorice.
Do you know all about your pal's likes and dislikes?

1. The three things my friend likes best about herself are . . .

2. Her most prized possession is her . . .

3. The best birthday present she could get is . . .

4. When she doodles, she is most likely to draw . . .

    a. cute puppies, kitties, or stick people.

    b. flowers, trees, a sun, or a moon.

    c. stars, arrows, hearts, or curlicues.

    d. triangles, boxes, or other geometric shapes.

13

5. Which of these things would she be *least* likely to do in front of other people?

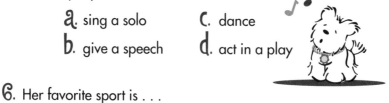

    a. sing a solo   **c.** dance

    b. give a speech   **d.** act in a play

6. Her favorite sport is . . .

----

7. Her favorite book is . . .

8. When it comes to snacking, she has . . .

    a. a sweet tooth.   **c.** salt attacks.

    b. healthy habits.   **d.** a spicy side.

9. Her favorite music group or singer is . . .

----

10. The one TV show that she never misses is . . .

----

11. She usually does her homework . . .

    a. in front of the TV.   **c.** in her room.

    b. at the kitchen table.   **d.** with me!

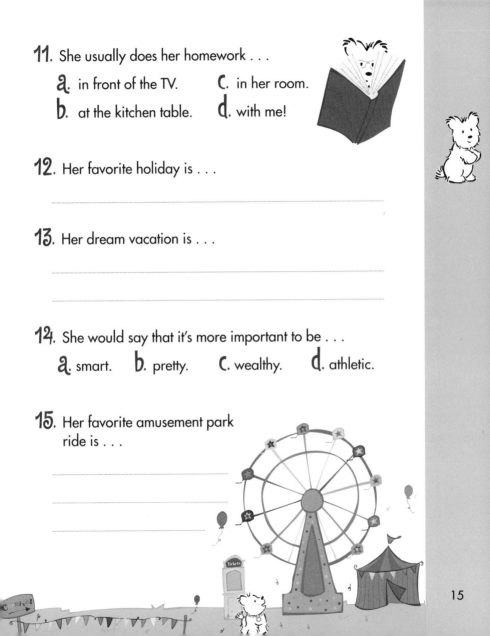

12. Her favorite holiday is . . .

_____

13. Her dream vacation is . . .

_____

_____

14. She would say that it's more important to be . . .

    a. smart.   **b.** pretty.   **c.** wealthy.   **d.** athletic.

15. Her favorite amusement park ride is . . .

_____

_____

_____

Answers

Now, have your friend check your answers. She gives you one point for each correct answer.

10 to 15 points

Wow! You must have spent countless hours talking with your pal. The most important thing, though, is that you must be a great listener because you surely know a lot about her!

5 to 9 points

You know your friend really well, but you still discover something new every now and then. That's all part of the fun of becoming even better friends.

0 to 4 points

The best part about having a friend is getting to know her better. The more time you spend together, the better you will get to know her!

Are You a Faithful Friend?

Coconut is a loyal pup through thick and thin. Are you? Take this quiz to find out.

1. Your friend told you a secret. You promised to keep quiet, but telling your sister doesn't count, does it? You spill the beans to your sister and ask her not to breathe a word.

   a. That's me!   **b.** I might do this.   **c.** I'd never do this.

2. You promised a friend that you'd help watch her little brother this Saturday, but another friend just asked you to go to the movies—same day, same time. You tell your other friend that something came up and hit the show.

   a. That's me!   **b.** I might do this.   **c.** I'd never do this.

3. Your friend just left her lucky bracelet at your house, and she has a piano recital this afternoon. You could run over to her house and return it, but you decide to wear it until you see her in school on Monday.

   a. That's me!   b. I might do this.   c. I'd never do this.

4. Oops! Something green from today's lunch has wedged itself between your friend's two front teeth. She looks so silly that you decide not to tell her.

   a. That's me!   b. I might do this.   c. I'd never do this.

5. Your friend's at camp, and you can tell by her postcard that she's homesick. Just as you start to write her back, your neighbor asks you to go swimming. You put off writing back to your friend until tomorrow.

   a. That's me!

   b. I might do this.

   c. I'd never do this.

Answers

If you answered **a** more than once,
you're a **Fair-Weather Friend**.

When skies are sunny, your friend can count on you. But when
clouds turn gray and she needs you, you're sometimes lost in a
fog. Put your friend first, and you'll both have brighter days
ahead!

If you answered mostly **b**'s,
you're a **Fickle Friend**.

In your heart, you know when it's time to put your friend's
needs before your own. But when it comes to following through,
you sometimes fall short. Try thinking of her feelings. You'll be
surprised by how good you'll feel when you do.

If you answered mostly **c**'s,
you're a **Faithful Friend**.

You and Coconut are two of a kind—loyal friends with lots of
heart. Let your friends down? No way. You've earned their trust,
and they know they can count on you no matter what.

A good friend is the cat's meow!

Sound Off

Coconut believes in speaking up, but she also knows that sometimes a loud bark just won't do. Knowing when to grin or growl isn't always easy. Take this quiz to find out where you fall on the bark-ometer.

1. You and your friends are deciding which movie to watch. They've chosen a scary one that's guaranteed to give you nightmares. You . . .

   a. let them watch it and try to look away when scary parts come.

   b. confess that this one's too much for you and ask if they wouldn't mind picking another.

   c. exclaim, "No way! This one is way better," as you pop in your favorite movie.

2. Your sister blames you for a scratch on her favorite CD. It was already there when you borrowed it. You . . .

a. say, "I probably did it. I'm sorry."

b. explain that the scratch was already there.

c. shout, "It's your stupid CD, and you scratched it!"

3. Some of your friend's classmates are teasing your friend about being the teacher's pet. You . . .

a. don't say anything, hoping they'll stop.

b. talk to your friend afterward and encourage her to stick up for herself.

c. tell the bullies, "You're just mad that she can do everything better than you!"

4. House rule: don't eat on the sofa. Your brother broke the rule and spilled grape juice on the cushion. He covered it up with a pillow, and your mom just walked in the door. You . . .

a. stay out of it.

b. pull your brother aside and encourage him to 'fess up.

c. exclaim, "Sam spilled grape juice on the couch!" before your mom has taken off her coat.

5. Your friend had a birthday party last spring and didn't invite you. Now it's your birthday. You . . .

a. invite her to your party without hesitation.

b. ask her why you weren't invited to her party, but invite her to yours anyway.

c. tell her she's not invited to your party.

Answers

Mostly a's
Bow-wow

You lie low and are quick to apologize. Don't be afraid to speak up for yourself, though.

Mostly b's
Woof!

You usually know when it's O.K. to let your feelings be known.

Mostly c's
Rrruff!

Sometimes a bark can be worse than a bite. Think before you speak.

Friendships bring sweet surprises.

Taste Test

Coconut loves treats! What makes *your* tastebuds sing? Answer these questions to see.

1. You have one quarter, and you're standing in front of three snack machines. You choose . . .

   a. peanuts.

   b. a giant sour ball.

   c. M&M's.

2. You're home from school and ready to have a snack. You grab . . .

   a. potato chips.

   b. a pickle.

   c. a chocolate chip cookie.

50 lb Size!

Doggy Puffs

3. You're about to see a movie, but first you head to the snack counter. You choose . . .

   a. popcorn.

   b. Sour Patch Kids.

   c. Milk Duds.

4. Your mouth waters most when you're licking . . .

   a. the salt off a pretzel.

   b. a lemon lollipop.

   c. the inside of an Oreo.

5. Your perfect Sunday morning breakfast has to have . . .

   a. bacon.

   b. grapefruit.

   c. donuts.

6. Your class won a pizza party for good behavior! You grab a slice of . . .

   a. pepperoni pizza.

   b. pineapple and ham pizza.

   c. dessert pizza with chocolate on top.

7. You're at a football game, and halftime means snack time! You get . . .

   a. a hot dog.

   b. sour gummy worms.

   c. cotton candy.

Answers

Mostly a's
SALTY

Your mouth waters over salty treats! Bland just won't do for you. But remember, too much salt isn't good for you. Go easy with the salty stuff, and let your great personality spice things up!

Mostly b's
SOUR

Extra pickles, please! They make you pucker, but that won't hold you back! With your taste for sour power, you're not afraid to try new things. And when life hands you lemons, you eat them!

Mostly c's
SWEET

Your favorite treats are super sweet, just like you! Next time your tummy's grumbling, grab a naturally sweet snack—like an apple or some grapes—to satisfy your sweet tooth.

A Good Night's Sleep

Coconut loves to snuggle up in a warm spot. How do you like to sleep? Check your favorite position. Then turn the page to find out what that says about you.

☐ **1.** Curled up on your side and holding your pillow

☐ **2.** On your side with legs and arms down

☐ **3.** On your side with legs down and arms raised

☐ **4.** On your back with legs and arms stretched out

☐ **5.** On your tummy with hands by your head

☐ **6.** Flat on your back with your arms at your sides

Answers

Here's what your sleeping position might say about you.

1. **Sleeping like a baby:** You sleep curled up on your side and holding your pillow. You are sensitive and sometimes shy.

2. **Dog tired:** If you sleep on your side with your legs and arms down, you are easygoing and love people.

3. **The big stretch:** If you sleep on your side with your legs down and your arms raised, you tend to be careful, and people need to earn your trust.

4. **Pooped pooch:** If you sleep on your back with your legs and arms stretched out, you're a good listener, and people like to be your friend.

5. **Happy camper:** You sleep on your tummy with your hands by your head. You're confident and friendly.

6. **You're back!** If you sleep flat on your back with your arms at your sides, you are quiet and you set high goals for yourself.

Which Popular Pet Are You?

Which famous pet are you most like? Pick a winner from each pair, and keep choosing until you've narrowed it down to your top dog—or cat!

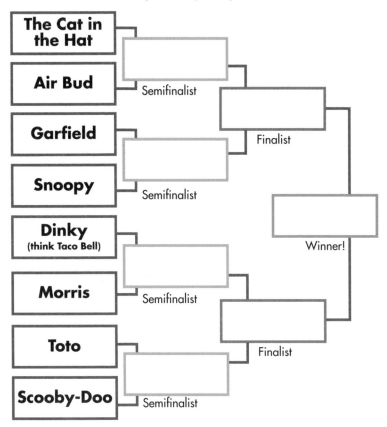

The Cat in the Hat

Air Bud

Semifinalist

Garfield

Snoopy

Semifinalist

Finalist

Dinky
(think Taco Bell)

Morris

Semifinalist

Winner!

Toto

Scooby-Doo

Semifinalist

Finalist

If you picked . . .

The Cat in the Hat, you're really clever and a bit mischievous. Plus, you love to rhyme . . . all the time!

Air Bud, you're like a golden retriever—friendly and devoted.

Garfield, you're a funny character. You have a sense of sarcasm, but deep down, you're a softy.

Snoopy, you're like a beagle—lovable and affectionate.

Dinky, you're like a Chihuahua—alert and curious.

Morris, you have style and personality, though you can be a bit finicky.

Toto, you're like a terrier—clever and full of energy.

Scooby-Doo, you're not a purebred but not a mutt. One thing's for sure—you're a #1 friend!

Pal Predictions

What does your friend want to be like when she grows up? Read this quiz with your friend in mind and guess which answer she'd pick for herself.

1. What kind of car does she drive?

   a. a green VW Beetle

   b. a sporty black pickup, to tote around all her pets

   c. a shiny red sports car—convertible, of course!

   d. a limousine, but *she* doesn't drive it—her chauffeur does

2. After high school, the first thing she plans to do is . . .

   a. go to college.

   b. start a rock band.

   c. travel the world.

   d. train for the Olympics.

3. The home of her dreams is . . .

   a. not a house—but a motor home, so she can cruise from place to place!

   b. a two-story with a white picket fence and a big yard.

   c. a loft apartment in a big city.

4. What's your friend's dream job?

   a. a world-famous artist

   b. a top-notch TV reporter

   c. a wildlife expert who saves endangered animals

   d. a hardworking lawyer who knows when she's right!

5. If you peeked in her fridge, what would you find?

   a. tons of takeout containers

   b. fresh fruits and veggies

   c. ice cream, chocolate milk, and hot dogs

6. If she could have one wish, what would it be?

   a. to record a top-ten hit song

   b. to make a world-changing scientific discovery

   c. to sail around the world

   d. to win the lottery

7. On Saturdays, where will your friend usually hang out?

    a. the movie theater

    b. any sporting event

    c. an art museum

    d. the beach—from sunrise to sunset!

Scoring

Now, have your friend check your answers. She gives you one point for each correct answer.

Total _____

Two Peas in a Pod

Take this quiz with your best bud to find out how well you really know each other.

1. If your friend could change her first name, she'd call

   herself ....

   You'd choose to go by ....

2. When she grows up, she wants to be a ....

   You want to be a ....

3. Your friend's room usually looks like . . .

   a. a hotel room.
   b. a natural disaster.

   What about your room? a.   b.

37

4. Which treat makes your friend's tail wag?

   a. brownies

   b. popcorn with extra butter

   Which snack do you sneak?   **a. b.**

5. At the video store, your friend would probably rent . . .

   a. *Spy Kids.*   **b.** *Finding Nemo.*   **c.** *The Princess Diaries.*

   What about you?   **a. b. c.**

6. Your friend would like to work on her science fair project . . .

   a. with you and a group of girls.

   b. by herself.

   How do you like to work?   **a. b.**

7. Which ice cream flavor is most like your friend?

   a. Rocky Road—sweet on the inside with lots of surprises!

   b. Vanilla—tried and true. You can always count on her!

   c. Rainbow Sherbet—always fun and colorful!

   Which flavor fits you?   **a. b. c.**

8. What is your friend's good-luck charm? ....

....

What's yours? ....

9. Have you or your friend ever . . .
jumped off a diving board?

Your friend .... You ....

changed a diaper?

Your friend .... You ....

traveled outside the United States?

Your friend .... You ....

seen the same movie three days in a row?

Your friend .... You ....

10. Your friend is most afraid of ....

What are you most afraid of?

....

Scoring

You get one point for each correct answer you gave about your friend. Your friend gets one point for each correct answer she gave about you. Add the scores together and check the chart.

Pal Points

6–12 points

Friends in Bloom

You don't know everything about each other—but you do know you can count on your friendship.

0–5 points

Getting to Know You

You've still got a lot to learn about each other—but that's what makes friendship fun!

13–19 points

Love Ya Like a Sister

You know each other so well, you're practically related!

20–26 points

BFF

You know what your friend is going to say before she says it— but you're such good pals, you love listening anyway.

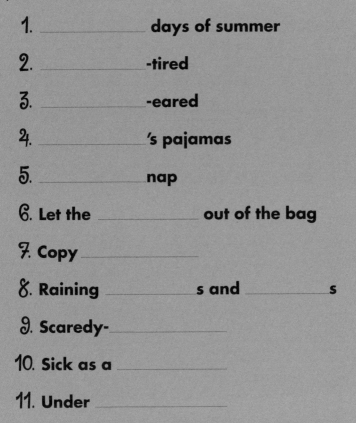

Speak!

Dogs and cats show up in some of the silliest places.
Fill in each phrase below with a "dog" or a "cat."
If you get all the correct answers, give yourself a
special treat!

1. _____ days of summer

2. _____-tired

3. _____-eared

4. _____'s pajamas

5. _____ nap

6. Let the _____ out of the bag

7. Copy _____

8. Raining _____ s and _____ s

9. Scaredy-_____

10. Sick as a _____

11. Under _____

41

Answers

1. **Dog days of summer**—those hot days in July and August when you don't feel like doing anything but lying around

2. **Dog-tired**—worn out, really tired

3. **Dog-eared**—folded-down corners of pages in a book

4. **Cat's pajamas**—something *especially* special

5. **Catnap**—a short rest, because cats can sleep anytime, anywhere!

6. **Let the cat out of the bag**—to tell a secret when you shouldn't

7. **Copycat**—copying someone's moves, like a kitten learns by copying her mother

8. **Raining cats and dogs**—it's raining really hard

9. **Scaredy-cat**—someone who's afraid, like cats usually are of dogs!

10. **Sick as a dog**—really, really sick

11. **Underdog**—someone who isn't expected to do well

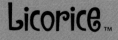

Quizzes

for a
Friend

The sweetest treat is the smile of a friend.

Favorite Flavors

Licorice's favorite flavor of ice cream is Licorice Kisses. Do you know what flavor is your friend's top pick? What about her least-likely-to-lick? Rank each flavor below for your friend from first (#1) to worst (#6).

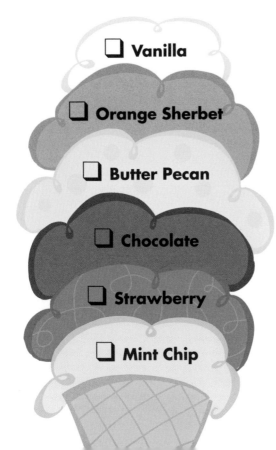

☐ **Vanilla**

☐ **Orange Sherbet**

☐ **Butter Pecan**

☐ **Chocolate**

☐ **Strawberry**

☐ **Mint Chip**

Answers

Ask your friend to check your answers to see how you did.
How many did you guess right?

One or two
Double Scoop Troop

There's plenty of time to learn more about each other. Why not
spend an afternoon sharing stories about yourselves—
while you share an ice cream sundae!

Three or four
Banana Split Sisters

You know a lot about your friend. But
she still likes to surprise you sometimes.
So many flavors, so little time!

Five or six
Whipped Cream Team

Your friend has no secrets from you—
or have you two been to the ice cream
shoppe together lately?

Dream On!

Sweet dreams? Not always. Dreams can also be silly, strange, or scary. Sometimes they represent what you're thinking or feeling. Check off any dreams below that you've had. Then read on to find out what your dreams might mean.

☐ **1. You're falling.**

☐ **2. You lost something.**

☐ **3. You're being chased.**

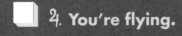 4. You're flying.

5. A house

 6. You're not wearing any clothes.

7. All your teeth fall out.

 8. A storm

BooM

Answers

1. You're falling.

Dreams of falling often mean that you're feeling uneasy or that someone has let you down. But did you know that people usually wake up before they hit bottom in their dreams?

2. You lost something.

If you dreamed about losing something, or if you were lost, you might be feeling like something is missing in your life. What do you think the lost item stands for?

3. You're being chased.

If you were running from something in a dream, chances are, you're trying to get away from something in your life. Have you been putting off some chores, or did you forget to do your homework?

4. You're flying.

How did you feel in your dream? If you felt happy, you're probably feeling on top of the world in real life. But if you were frightened in your dream, there might be something scary you wish you could run from—like that upcoming piano recital!

5. A house

The house represents you. Was there a hidden room? Maybe you're keeping a secret in real life. Were the rooms all different colors? Maybe you have a flair for art or fashion.

6. You're not wearing any clothes.

Dreams about being naked have to do with your feelings— *not* your body. Perhaps in real life, there's a thought or feeling that you'd like to keep under wraps?

7. All your teeth fall out.

This dream may seem weird, but lots of people have it. Usually, it means there's something in your life that feels out of your control. Maybe your room is super messy, or your little brother has been bugging you.

8. A storm

Dreams about natural disasters are scary. They usually represent something in your life that is frightening you, too. A tornado, for example, may mean you're feeling out of control.

Here's to sweet dreams and starry skies!

Pal Poll

Licorice knows a lot about her friend Coconut.
Do you know all about your pal's likes and dislikes?

1. The three things my friend likes best about herself are . . .

2. Her most prized possession is her . . .

3. The best birthday present she could get is . . .

4. When she doodles, she is most likely to draw . . .

a. cute puppies, kitties, or stick people

b. flowers, trees, a sun, or a moon

C. stars, arrows, hearts, or curlicues

d. triangles, boxes, or other geometric shapes

5. Which of these things would she be *least* likely to do in front of other people?

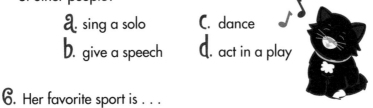

a. sing a solo   C. dance

b. give a speech   d. act in a play

6. Her favorite sport is . . .

7. Her favorite book is . . .

8. When it comes to snacking, she has . . .

a. a sweet tooth.   C. salt attacks.

b. healthy habits.   d. a spicy side.

9. Her favorite music group or singer is . . .

10. The one TV show that she never misses is . . .

11. She usually does her homework . . .

    a. in front of the TV.   **C.** in her room.

    b. at the kitchen table.   **d.** with me!

12. Her favorite holiday is . . .

_____

13. Her dream vacation is . . .

_____

_____

14. She would say that it's more important to be . . .

    a. smart.   **b.** pretty.   **C.** wealthy.   **d.** athletic.

15. Her favorite amusement park ride is . . .

_____

_____

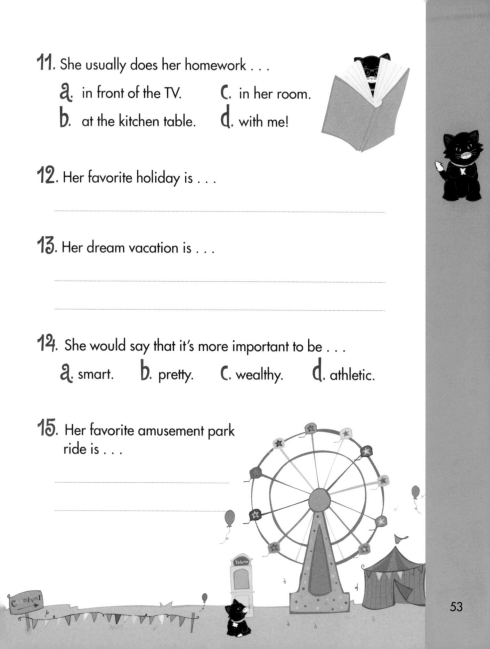

Answers

Now, have your friend check your answers. She gives you one point for each correct answer.

10 to 15 points

Wow! You must have spent countless hours talking with your pal. The most important thing, though, is that you must be a great listener because you surely know a lot about her!

5 to 9 points

You know your friend really well, but you still discover something new every now and then. That's all part of the fun of becoming even better friends.

0 to 4 points

The best part about having a friend is getting to know her better. The more time you spend together, the better you will get to know her!

Are You a Faithful Friend?

Licorice is a dedicated kitty through thick and thin.
Are you? Take this quiz to find out.

1. Your friend told you a secret. You promised to keep quiet, but telling your sister doesn't count, does it? You spill the beans to your sister and ask her not to breathe a word.

   a. That's me!   b. I might do this.   c. I'd never do this.

2. You promised a friend that you'd help watch her little brother this Saturday, but another friend just asked you to go to the movies—same day, same time. You tell your other friend that something came up and hit the show.

   a. That's me!   b. I might do this.   c. I'd never do this.

55

3. Your friend just left her lucky bracelet at your house, and she has a piano recital this afternoon. You could run over to her house and return it, but you decide to wear it until you see her in school on Monday.

   a. That's me!   b. I might do this.   c. I'd never do this.

4. Oops! Something green from today's lunch has wedged itself between your friend's two front teeth. She looks so silly that you decide not to tell her.

   a. That's me!   b. I might do this.   c. I'd never do this.

5. Your friend's at camp, and you can tell by her postcard that she's homesick. Just as you start to write her back, your neighbor asks you to go swimming. You put off writing back to your friend until tomorrow.

   a. That's me!

   b. I might do this.

   c. I'd never do this.

Answers

If you answered **a** more than once,
you're a **Fair-Weather Friend**.

When skies are sunny, your friend can count on you. But when clouds turn gray and she needs you, you're sometimes lost in the fog. Put your friend first, and you'll both have brighter days ahead!

If you answered mostly **b**'s,
you're a **Fickle Friend**.

In your heart, you know when it's time to put your friend's needs before your own. But when it comes to following through, you sometimes fall short. Try thinking of her feelings. You'll be surprised by how good you'll feel when you do.

If you answered mostly **c**'s,
you're a **Faithful Friend**.

You and Licorice are two of a kind—loyal friends with lots of heart. Let your friends down? No way. You've earned their trust, and they know they can count on you no matter what.

A good friend is the cat's meow!

Sound Off

Licorice believes in speaking up, but she also knows that sometimes a proud meow just won't do. Knowing when to purr or hiss isn't always easy. Take this quiz to find out where you fall on the meow-ometer.

1. You and your friends are deciding which movie to watch. They've chosen a scary one that's guaranteed to give you nightmares. You . . .

   a. let them watch it and try to look away when scary parts come.

   b. confess that this one's too much for you and ask if they wouldn't mind picking another.

   c. exclaim, "No way! This one is way better," as you pop in your favorite movie.

2. Your sister blames you for a scratch on her favorite CD. It was already there when you borrowed it. You . . .

   a. say, "I probably did it. I'm sorry."

   b. explain that the scratch was already there.

   c. shout, "It's your stupid CD, and you scratched it!"

3. Some of your friend's classmates are teasing your friend about being the teacher's pet. You . . .

   a. don't say anything, hoping they'll stop.

   b. talk to your friend afterward and encourage her to stick up for herself.

   c. tell the bullies, "You're just mad that she can do everything better than you!"

4. House rule: don't eat on the sofa. Your brother broke the rule and spilled grape juice on the cushion. He covered it up with a pillow, and your mom just walked in the door. You . . .

   a. stay out of it.

   b. pull your brother aside and encourage him to 'fess up.

   c. exclaim, "Sam spilled grape juice on the couch!" before your mom has taken off her coat.

5. Your friend had a birthday party last spring and didn't invite you. Now it's your birthday. You . . .

a. invite her to your party without hesitation.

b. ask her why you weren't invited to her party, but invite her to yours anyway.

C. tell her she's not invited to your party.

Answers

Mostly a's
Mew!

You lie low and are quick to apologize. Don't be afraid to speak up for yourself, though.

Mostly b's
Purr-fect

You usually know when it's O.K. to let your feelings be known.

Mostly C's
Hiss!

Sometimes a kitty should be seen but not heard. Think before you speak.

Friendships bring sweet surprises.

Taste Test

Licorice loves treats! What makes *your* tastebuds sing? Answers these questions to see.

1. You have one quarter, and you're standing in front of three snack machines. You choose . . .

   a. peanuts.

   b. a giant sour ball.

   c. M&M's.

2. You're home from school and ready to have a snack. You grab . . .

   a. potato chips.

   b. a pickle.

   c. a chocolate chip cookie.

3. You're about to see a movie, but first you head to the snack counter. You choose . . .

   a. popcorn.

   b. Sour Patch Kids.

   C. Milk Duds.

4. Your mouth waters most when you're licking . . .

   a. the salt off a pretzel.

   b. a lemon lollipop.

   C. the inside of an Oreo.

5. Your perfect Sunday morning breakfast has to have . . .

   a. bacon.

   b. grapefruit.

   C. donuts.

6. Your class won a pizza party for good behavior! You grab a slice of . . .

   a. pepperoni pizza.

   b. pineapple and ham pizza.

   c. dessert pizza with chocolate on top.

7. You're at a football game, and halftime means snack time! You get . . .

   a. a hot dog.

   b. sour gummy worms.

   c. cotton candy.

Answers

Mostly a's
SALTY

Your mouth waters over salty treats! Bland just won't do for you. But remember, too much salt isn't good for you. Go easy with the salty stuff, and let your great personality spice things up!

Mostly b's
SOUR

Extra pickles, please! They make you pucker, but that won't hold you back! With your taste for sour power, you're not afraid to try new things. And when life hands you lemons, you eat them!

Mostly c's
SWEET

Your favorite treats are super sweet, just like you! Next time your tummy's grumbling, grab a naturally sweet snack—like an apple or some grapes—to satisfy your sweet tooth.

A Good Night's Sleep

Licorice loves to curl up in a warm spot. How do you like to sleep? Check your favorite position. Then turn the page to find out what that says about you.

☐ **1.** Curled up on your side and holding your pillow

☐ **2.** On your side with legs and arms down

☐ **3.** On your side with legs down and arms raised

☐ **4.** On your back with legs and arms stretched out

☐ **5.** On your tummy with hands by your head

☐ **6.** Flat on your back with your arms at your sides

Answers

Here's what your sleeping position might say about you.

1. **Sleeping like a baby:** You sleep curled up on your side and holding your pillow. You are sensitive and sometimes shy.

2. **Feline fine:** If you sleep on your side with your legs and arms down, you are easygoing and love people.

3. **The big stretch:** If you sleep on your side with your legs down and your arms raised, you tend to be careful, and people need to earn your trust.

4. **Cat's pajamas:** If you sleep on your back with your legs and arms stretched out, you're a good listener, and people like to be your friend.

5. **Happy camper:** You sleep on your tummy with your hands by your head. You're confident and friendly.

6. **You're back!** If you sleep flat on your back with your arms at your sides, you are quiet and you set high goals for yourself.

Which Popular Pet Are You?

Which famous pet are you most like? Pick a winner from each pair, and keep choosing until you've narrowed it down to your top dog—or cat!

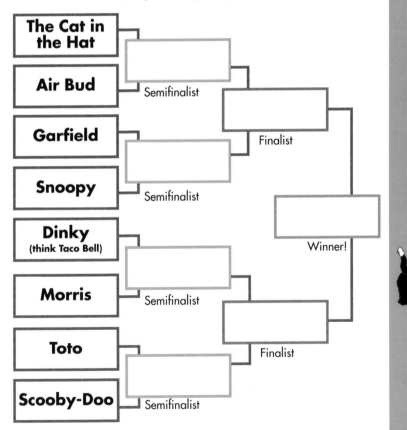

The Cat in the Hat

Air Bud

Semifinalist

Garfield

Snoopy

Semifinalist

Finalist

Dinky
(think Taco Bell)

Morris

Semifinalist

Winner!

Toto

Scooby-Doo

Semifinalist

Finalist

If you picked . . .

The Cat in the Hat, you're really clever and a bit mischievous. Plus, you love to rhyme . . . all the time!

Air Bud, you're like a golden retriever—friendly and devoted.

Garfield, you're a funny character. You have a sense of sarcasm, but deep down, you're a softy.

Snoopy, you're like a beagle—lovable and affectionate.

Dinky, you're like a Chihuahua—alert and curious.

Morris, you have style and personality, though you can be a bit finicky.

Toto, you're like a terrier—clever and full of energy.

Scooby-Doo, you're not a purebred but not a mutt. One thing's for sure—you're a #1 friend!

Pal Predictions

What does your friend want to be like when she grows up? Read this quiz with your friend in mind and guess which answer she'd pick for herself.

1. What kind of car does she drive?

   a. a green VW Beetle

   b. a sporty black pickup, to tote around all her pets

   c. a shiny red sports car—convertible, of course!

   d. a limousine, but *she* doesn't drive it—her chauffeur does

2. After high school, the first thing she plans to do is . . .

   a. go to college.

   b. start a rock band.

   c. travel the world.

   d. train for the Olympics.

3. The home of her dreams is . . .

    a. not a house—but a motor home, so she can cruise from place to place!

    b. a two-story with a white picket fence and a big yard.

    c. a loft apartment in a big city.

4. What's your friend's dream job?

    a. a world-famous artist

    b. a top-notch TV reporter

    c. a wildlife expert who saves endangered animals

    d. a hardworking lawyer who knows when she's right!

5. If you peeked in her fridge, what would you find?

   a. tons of takeout containers

   b. fresh fruits and veggies

   c. ice cream, chocolate milk, and hot dogs

6. If she could have one wish, what would it be?

   a. to record a top-ten hit song

   b. to make a world-changing scientific discovery

   c. to sail around the world

   d. to win the lottery

7. On Saturdays, where will your friend usually hang out?

    a. the movie theater

    b. any sporting event

    c. an art museum

    d. the beach—from sunrise to sunset!

Scoring

Now, have your friend check your answers. She gives you one point for each correct answer.

Total _____

Two Peas in a Pod

Take this quiz with your best bud to find out how well you really know each other.

1. If your friend could change her first name, she'd call

   herself...

   You'd choose to go by...

2. When she grows up, she wants to be a ....

   You want to be a ....

3. Your friend's room usually looks like . . .
   a. a hotel room.
   b. a natural disaster.

   What about your room? a. b.

4. Which treat makes your friend's tail wag?

   a. brownies

   b. popcorn with extra butter

   Which snack do you sneak?   a. b.

5. At the video store, your friend would probably rent . . .

   a. *Spy Kids.*   b. *Finding Nemo.*   c. *The Princess Diaries.*

   What about you?   a. b. c.

6. Your friend would like to work on her science fair project . . .

   a. with you and a group of girls.

   b. by herself.

   How do you like to work?   a. b.

7. Which ice cream flavor is most like your friend?

   a. Rocky Road—sweet on the inside with lots of surprises!

   b. Vanilla—tried and true. You can always count on her!

   c. Rainbow Sherbet—always fun and colorful!

   Which flavor fits you?   a. b. c.

8. What is your friend's good-luck charm? _____

_____

What's yours? _____

9. Have you or your friend ever . . .
jumped off a diving board?

      Your friend _____ You _____

changed a diaper?

      Your friend _____ You _____

traveled outside the United States?

      Your friend _____ You _____

seen the same movie three days in a row?

      Your friend _____ You _____

10. Your friend is most afraid of _____

What are you most afraid of?

_____

Scoring

You get one point for each correct answer you gave about your friend. Your friend gets one point for each correct answer she gave about you. Add the scores together and check the chart.

Pal Points

0–5 points

Getting to Know You

You've still got a lot to learn about each other—but that's what makes friendship fun!

6–12 points

Friends in Bloom

You don't know everything about each other—but you do know you can count on your friendship.

13–19 points

Love Ya Like a Sister

You know each other so well, you're practically related!

20–26 points

BFF

You know what your friend is going to say before she says it—but you're such good pals, you love listening anyway.

Speak!

Dogs and cats show up in some of the silliest places. Fill in each phrase below with a "dog" or a "cat." If you get all the correct answers, give yourself a special treat!

1. _____ days of summer

2. _____ -tired

3. _____ -eared

4. _____ 's pajamas

5. _____ nap

6. Let the _____ out of the bag

7. Copy _____

8. Raining _____ s and _____ s

9. Scaredy- _____

10. Sick as a _____

11. Under _____

Answers

1. **Dog days of summer**—those hot days in July and August when you don't feel like doing anything but lying around

2. **Dog-tired**—worn out, really tired

3. **Dog-eared**—folded-down corners of pages in a book

4. **Cat's pajamas**—something *especially* special

5. **Catnap**—a short rest, because cats can sleep anytime, anywhere!

6. **Let the cat out of the bag**—to tell a secret when you shouldn't

7. **Copycat**—copying someone's moves, like a kitten learns by copying her mother

8. **Raining cats and dogs**—it's raining really hard

9. **Scaredy-cat**—someone who's afraid, like cats usually are of dogs!

10. **Sick as a dog**—really, really sick

11. **Underdog**—someone who isn't expected to do well